I0468743

Farm Animals Coloring Book

Farm Adult Coloring Book, Advanced Coloring Books for Adults for Stress Relief and Relaxation

Realistic Animals Coloring Book: Vol 10

by Amanda Davenport

ISBN-13: 978-1530946389

ISBN-10: 1530946387

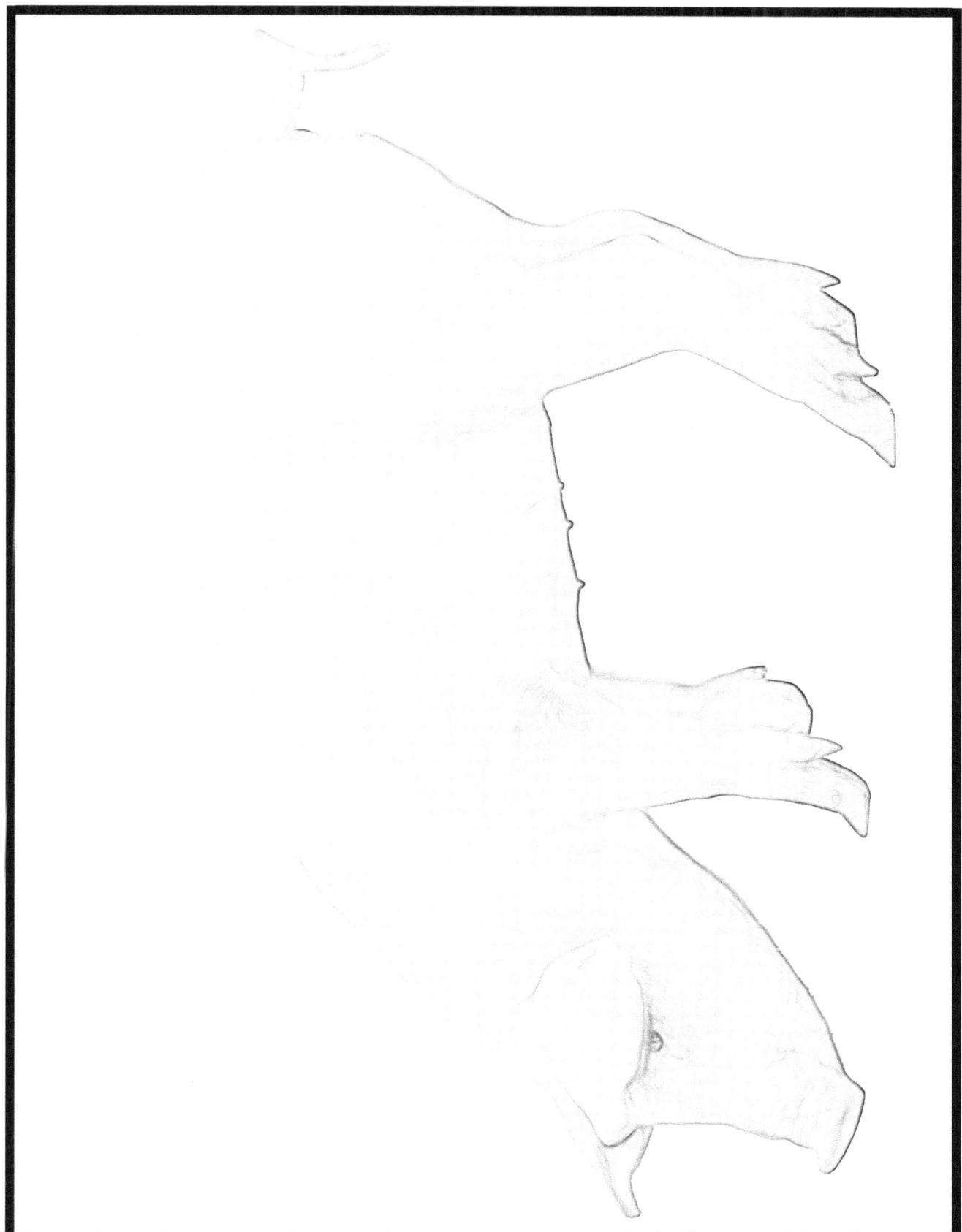

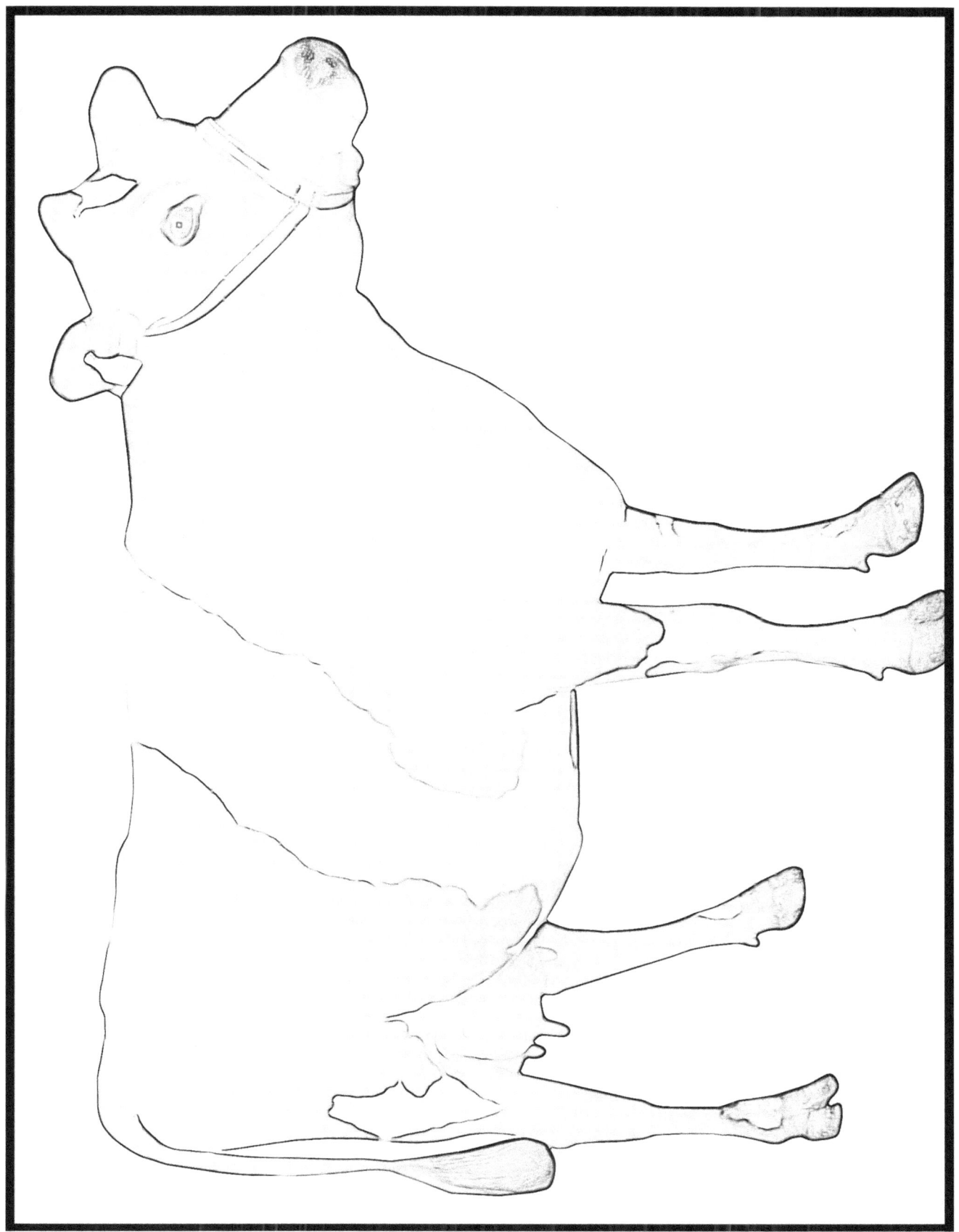

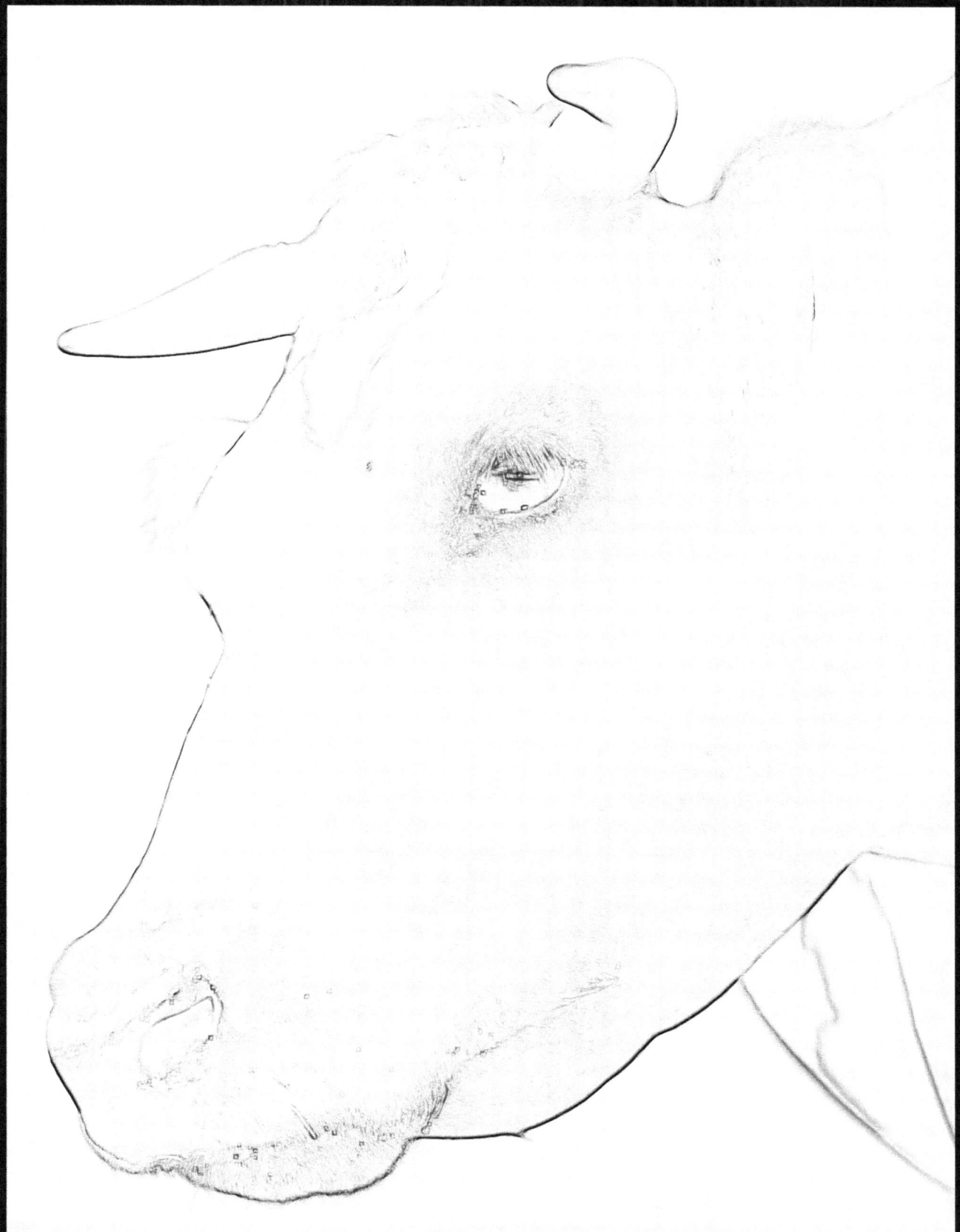

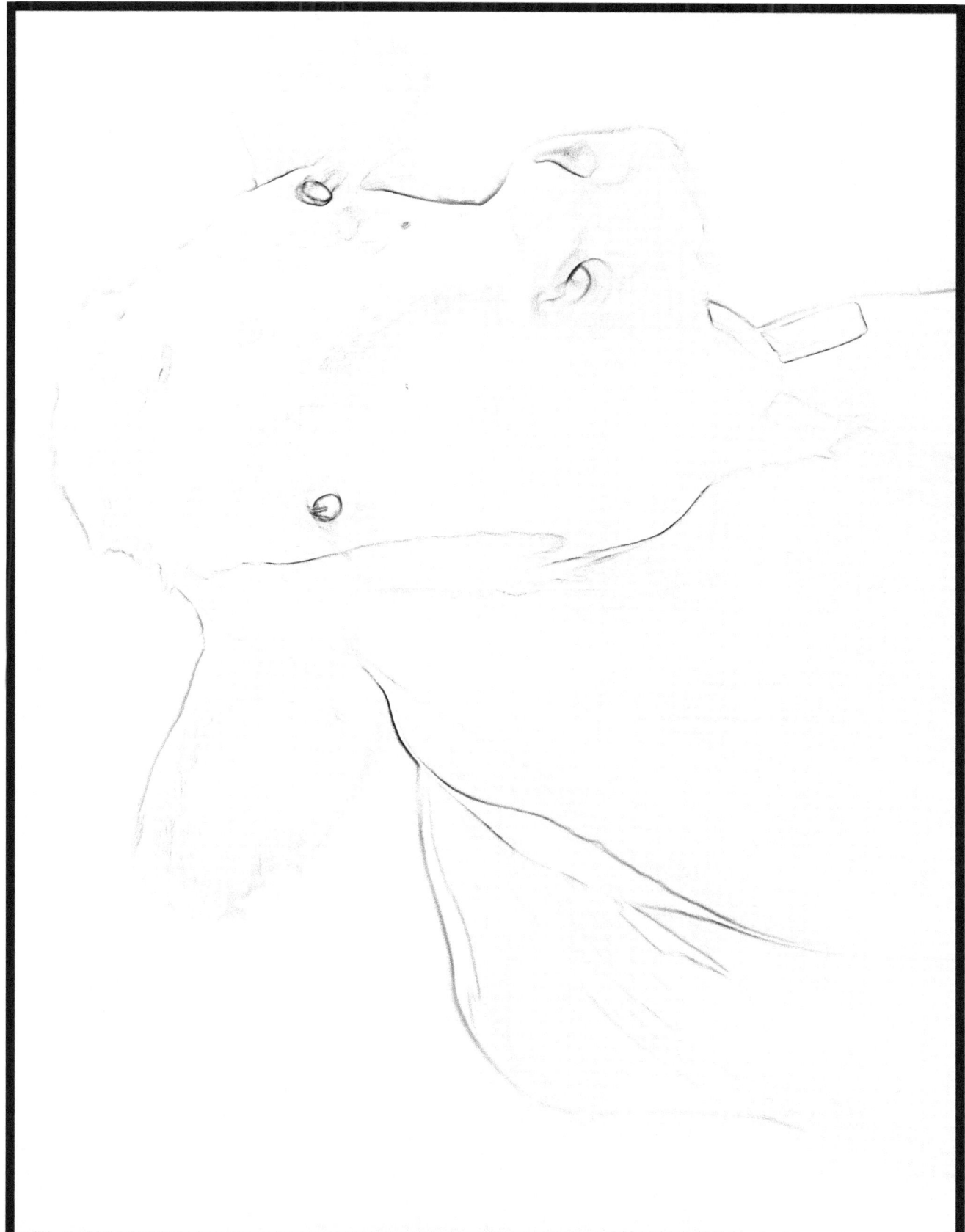

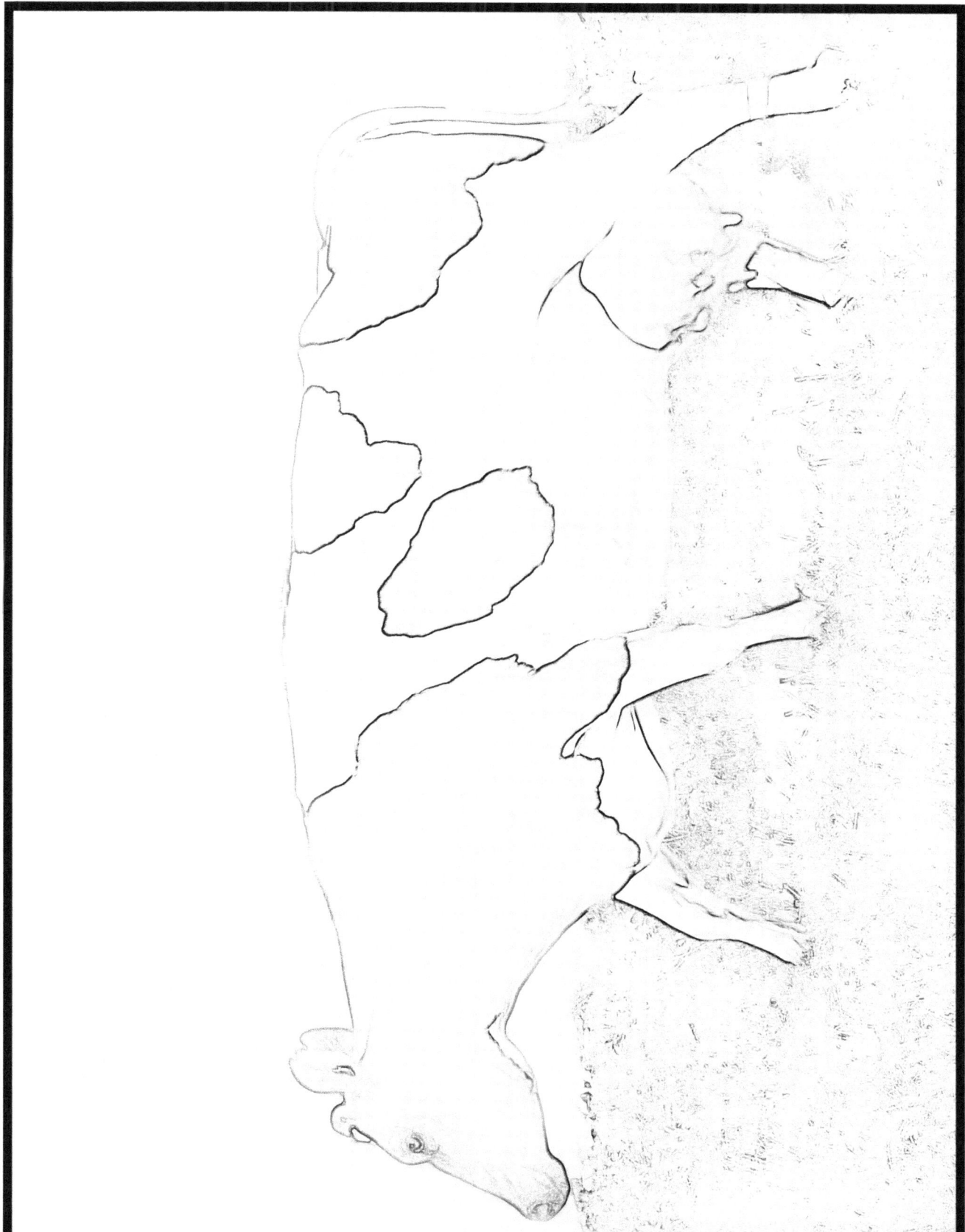

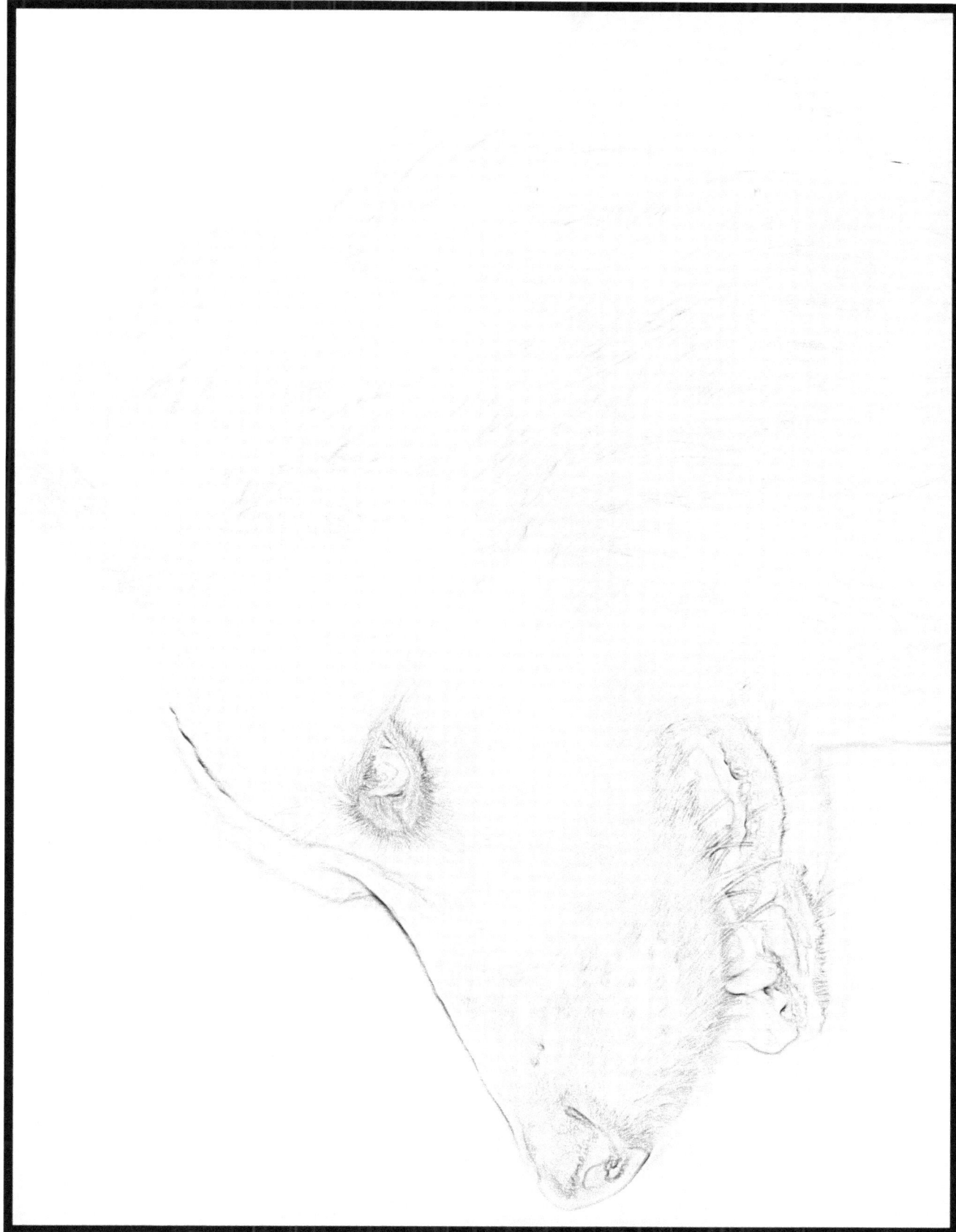

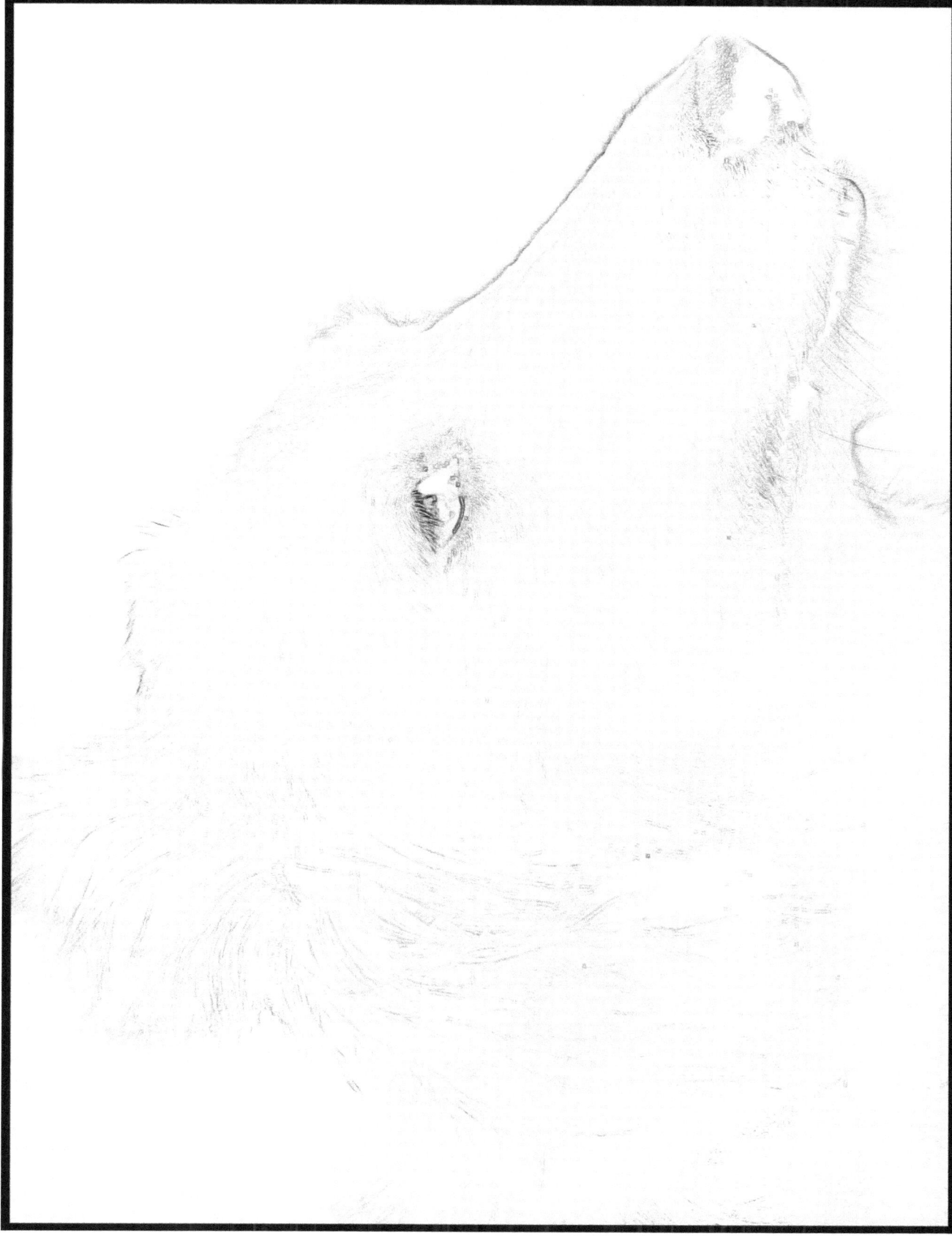

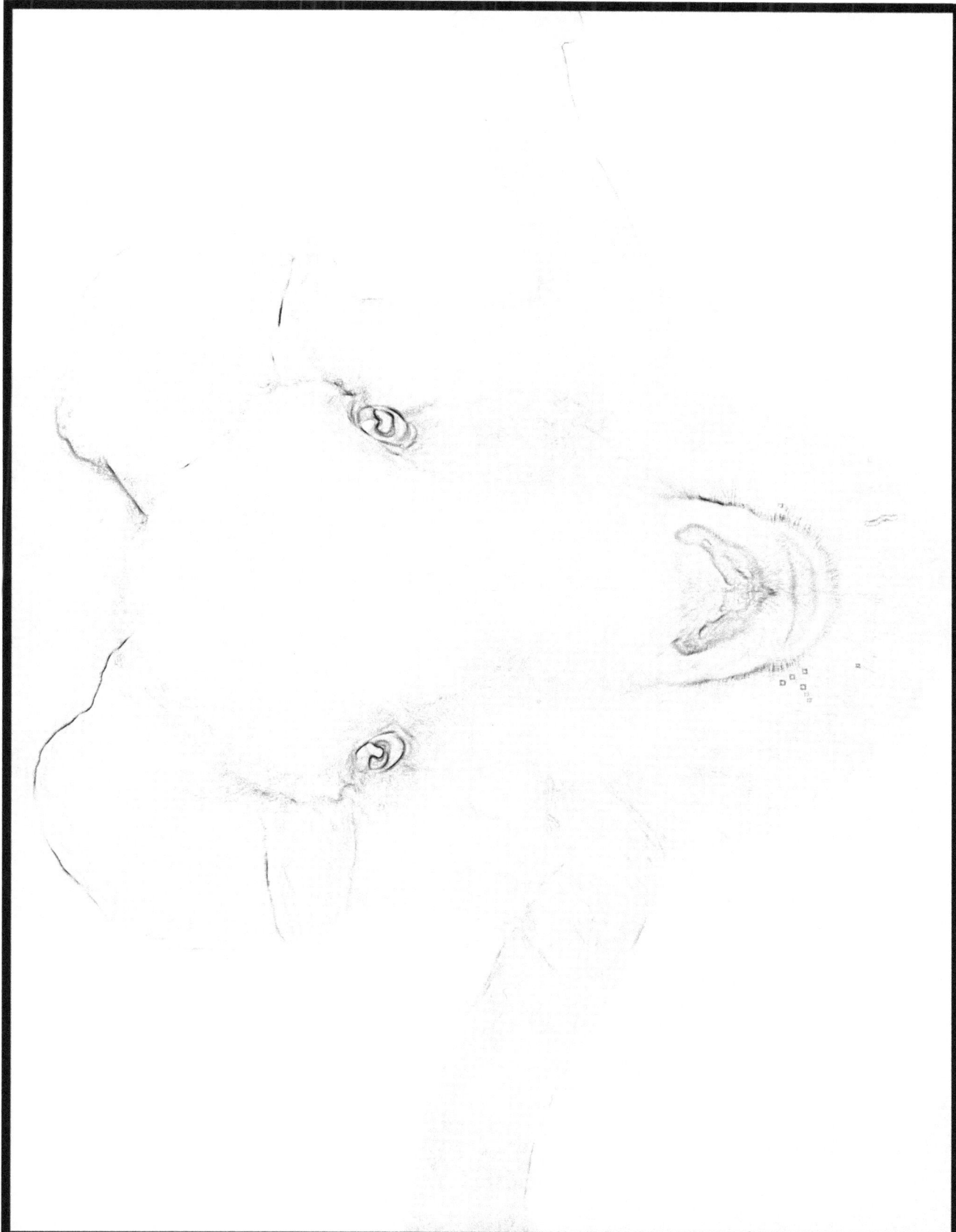

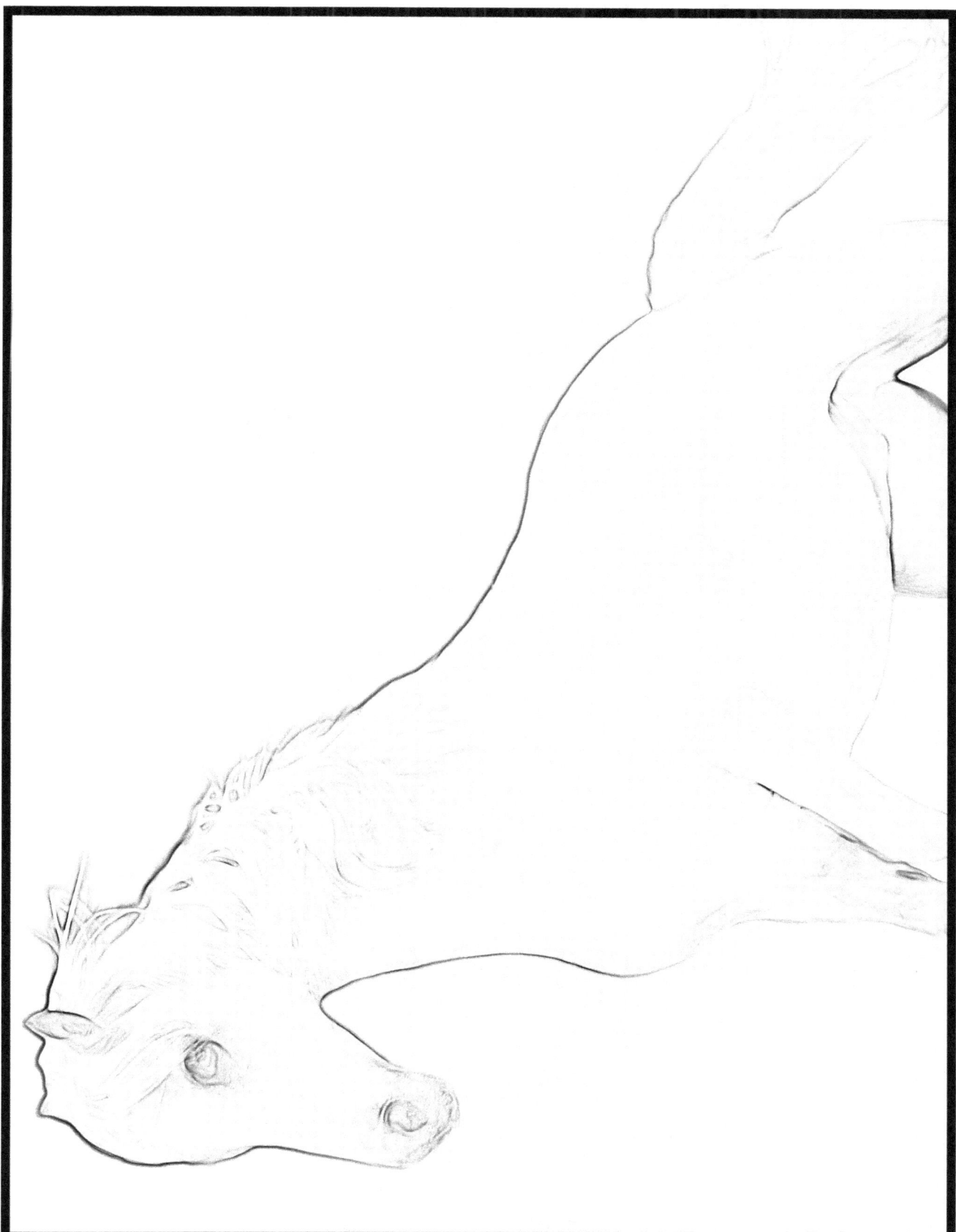

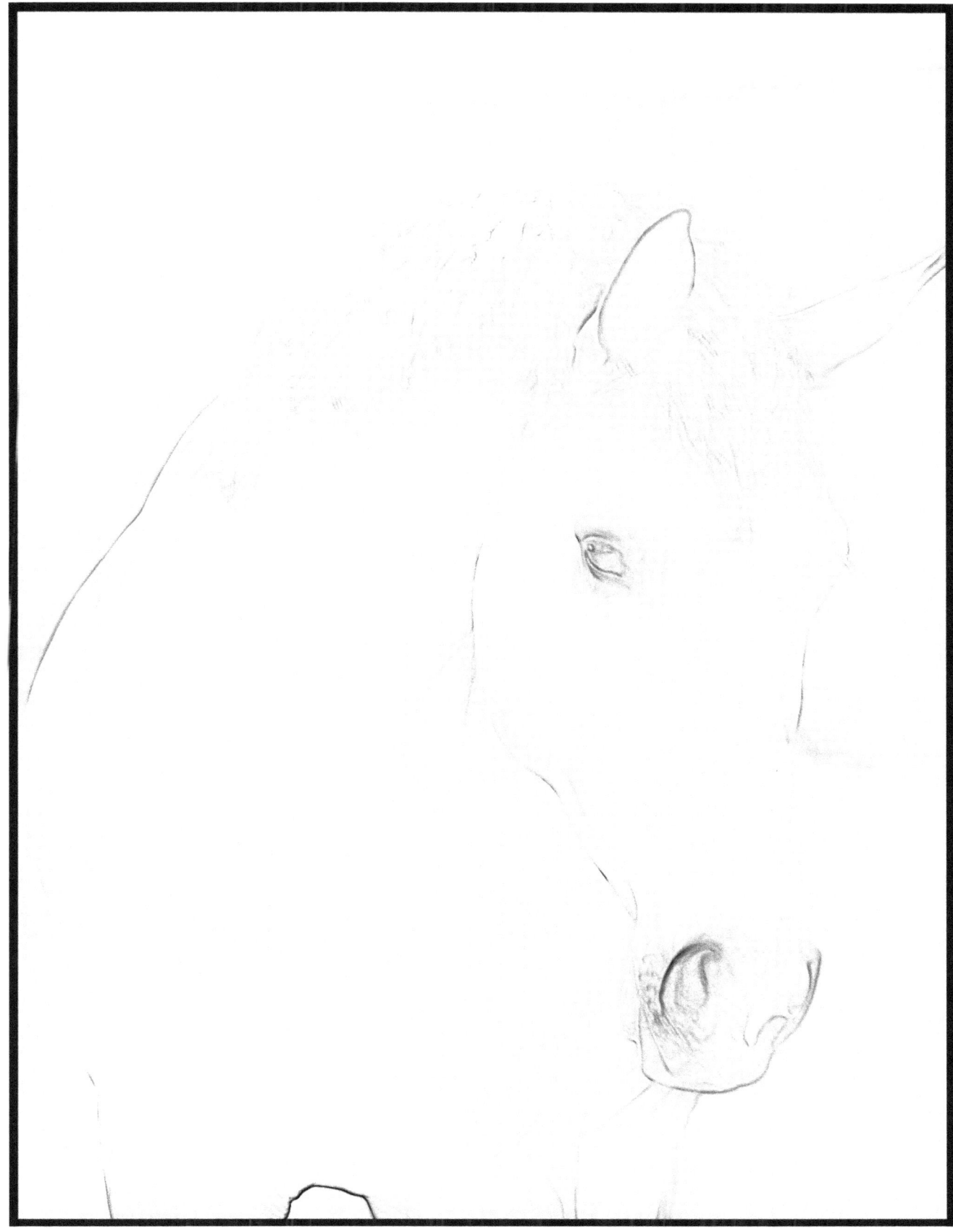

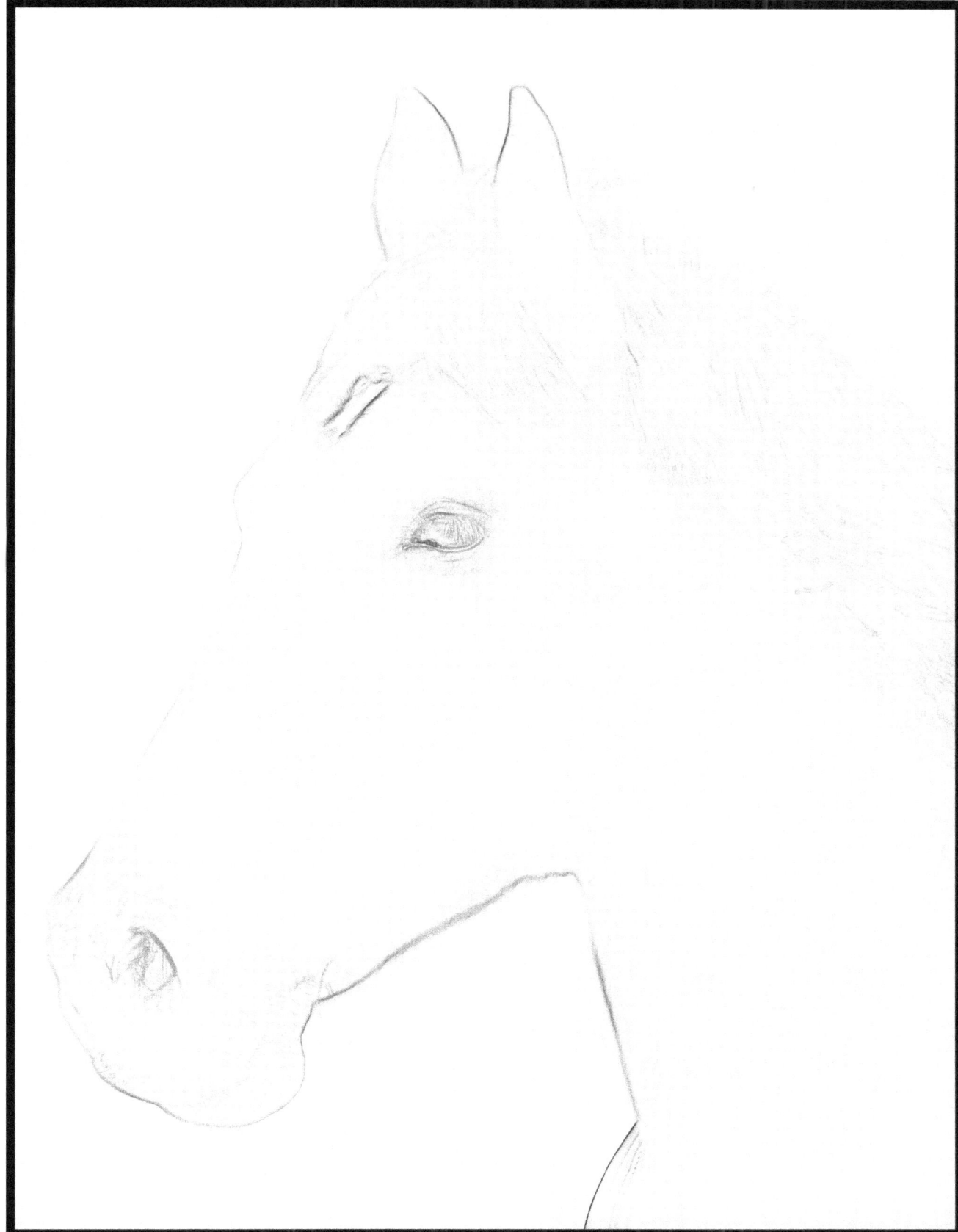

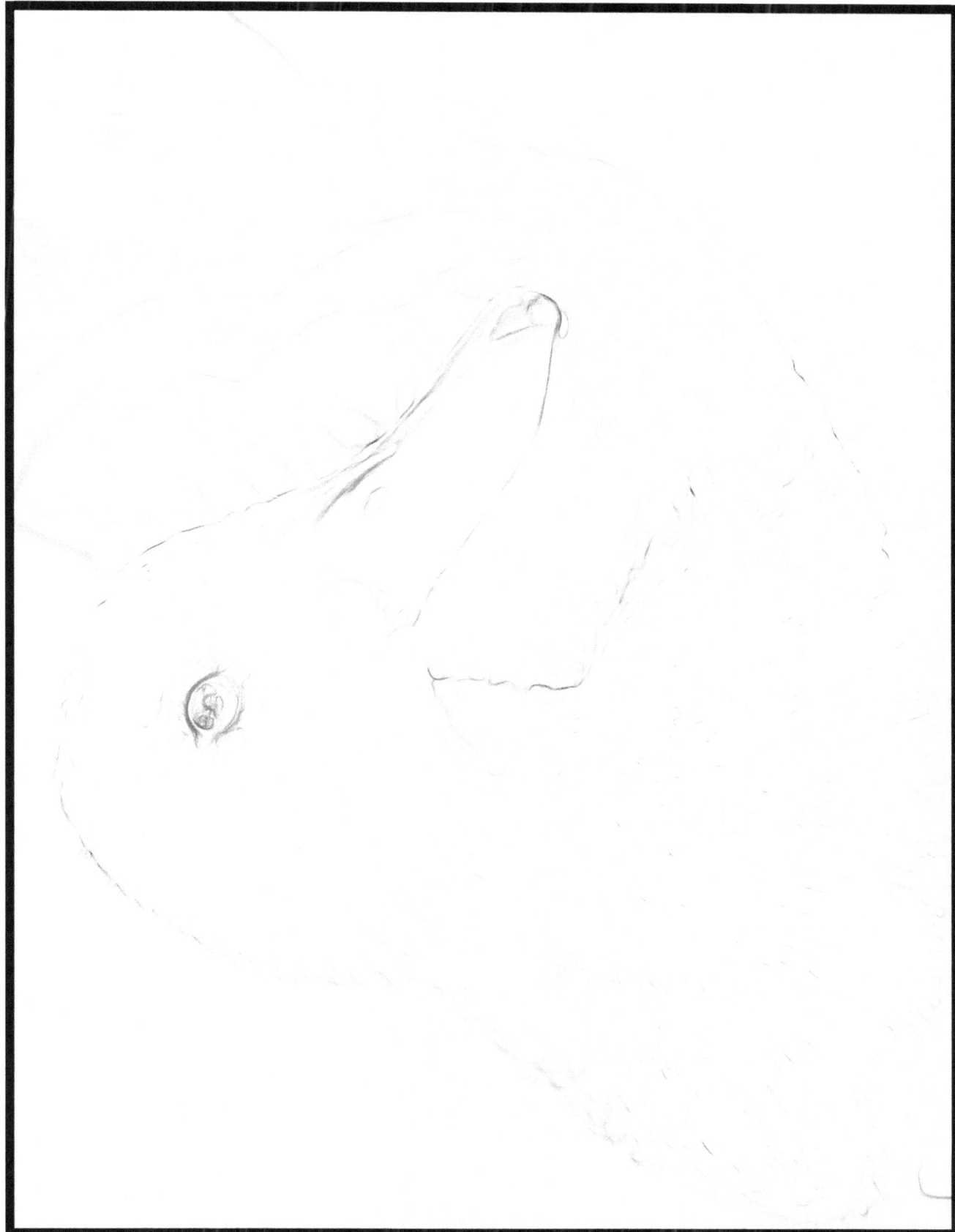

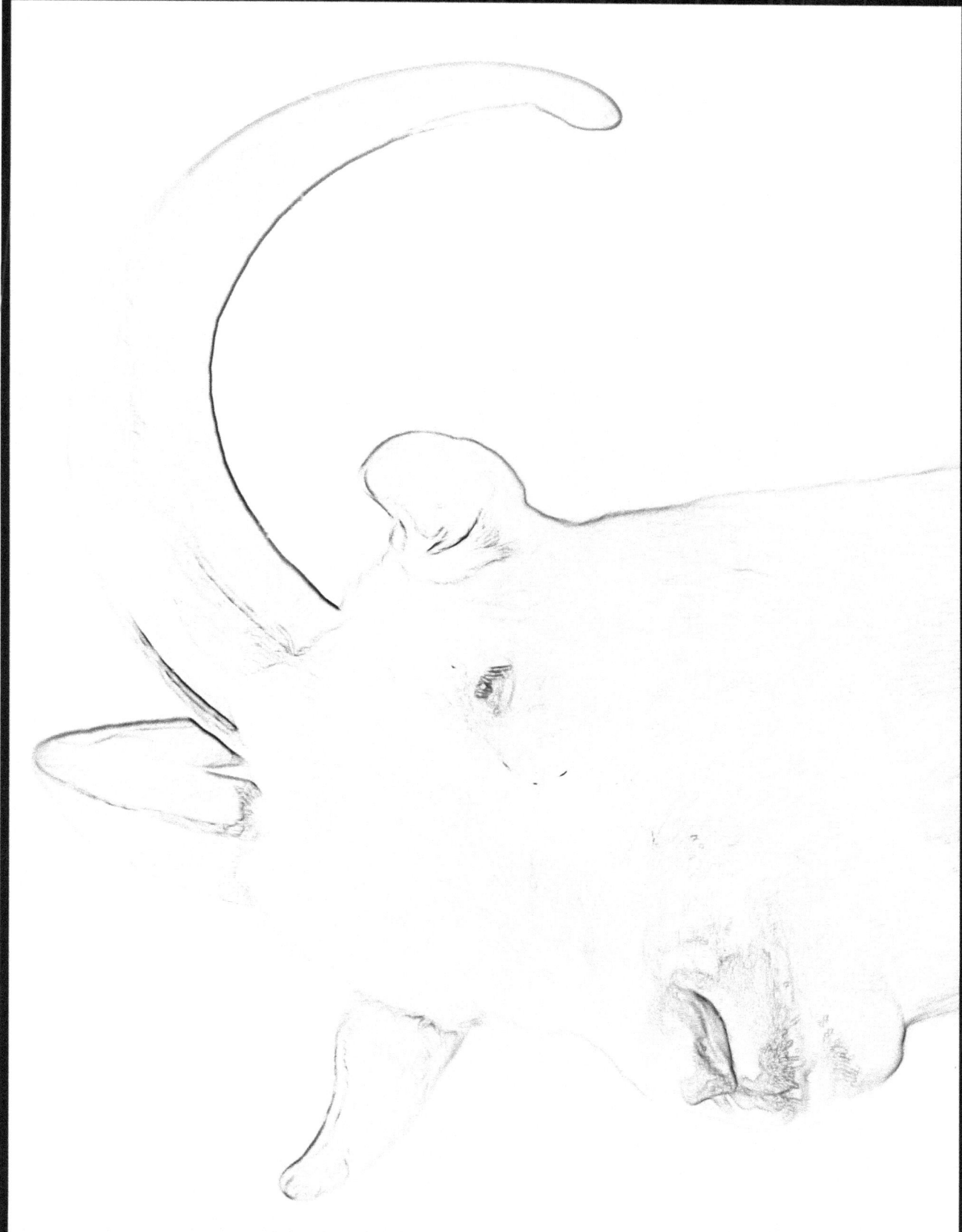

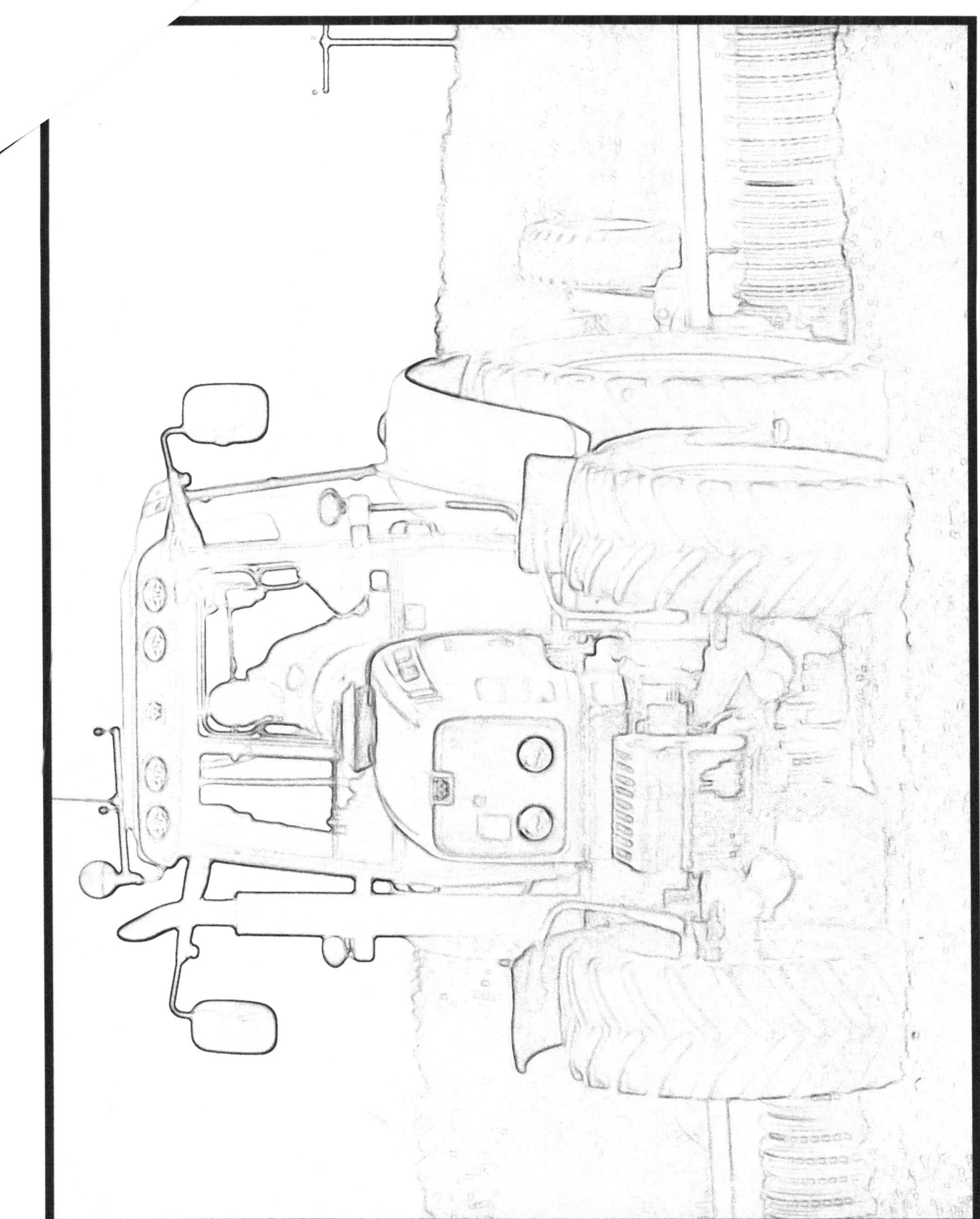